A WOMAN'S ODE TO MAN

Poems from A Woman's Perspective

Paula Love Clark

Author of the Best Selling *An Ode to Woman*

Disclaimer

This book is designed to provide information and motivation to our readers. It is sold with the understanding that the author and publisher are not engaged to render any type of psychological, legal, or any other kind of professional advice. The content is the sole expression and opinion of its author. Neither the publisher nor the individual author(s) shall be liable for any physical, psychological, emotional, financial, or commercial damages, including, but not limited to, special, incidental, consequential or other damages. Our views and rights are the same: You are responsible for your own choices, actions, and results.

The content of the book is solely written by the author.

DVG STAR Publishing are not liable for the content of the book.

Published by DVG STAR PUBLISHING

www.dvgstar.com

email us at info@dvgstar.com

NO PART OF THIS WORK MAY BE REPRODUCED OR STORED IN AN INFORMATIONAL RETRIEVAL SYSTEM, WITHOUT THE EXPRESS PERMISSION OF THE PUBLISHER IN WRITING.

DEDICATION

To my beautiful children Harriet, Lauren and Zac.

I write for you ♥

"What the essential difference between man and woman is, that they should be thus attracted to one another, no one has satisfactorily answered. Perhaps we must acknowledge the justness of the distinction which assigns to man the sphere of wisdom and to woman that of love, though neither belongs exclusively to either. Man is continually saying to woman, Why will you not be more wise? Woman is continually saying to man, Why will you not be more loving? It is not in their wills to be wise or to be loving; but, unless each is both wise and loving, there can be neither wisdom nor love."

- Henry David Thoreau

CONTENTS

'AN ODE TO MAN'

This woman does not know what it's like to be a man.

So in trying to understand, I'm exploring if we can,

Comprehend each other, so let's take a look at you,

But remember that it's coming from,

Just one 'bird's' eye point of view.

PART ONE
THE GUY STUFF

BOYS AND THEIR TOYS

THE SOUND OF THE VROOM VROOM

It must have started in the womb
That love of all things zoom and vroom
From cars and trucks and planes and bikes
These are things that most boys like.
And when the boys get all growed up
They go and get some bigger trucks.

TOM'S NEW CAR

Tom has got a shiny car
Better than his last
He shines it almost daily
And polishes the glass
The steering wheel is leather
And the trims are shining black
I guess now Tom is winning
Not living in the lack.

How I'd love to get a car
A shiny one like Tom adores
But I guess until I'm flush like him
I'll be driving my old Ford.

LITTLE BOYS

Do you think there is an Angel
Way high up in the sky,
Whose job it is to train the boys
To like blue and only try
Out all the many boys toys,
Like balls and cars and trucks,
And jump on all the sofas
Till your parents get the hump?

To always want to be,
Outside or in the park,
No matter what the weather
And up before the lark?
To not like having crusts,
On any kind of bread
And forever banging arms or knees,
Or often just their head?

To always want to come first;
last will never do
And fill their brand new wellies,
With sludge, or wee, or poo?
To play with tiny bugs
And never clean their teeth
Pretending that they've washed their hands
And wiped their underneath?

Little boys they can be testing
And push you to the edge,
But when it comes to love and hugs,
Little boys they are the best

ALL THINGS BALLS

Kicking, putting, batting,
Dribbling, whacking, patting,
Bouncing, hitting, pinging,
Scoring, beating, winning.

Is it because they have your own,
That guys like balls from babe to grown?
Is it something women won't know
Because we haven't had balls to hold?

Widows of the pitch all unite,
Against the ball delight.
Of men and boys
And all their ball sport obsessed noise.

SHED MAN

There is a place where man does go
A secret place for no woman you know.
A cave for men and tools and stuff
He goes there often when he's had enough
Of life, of things, people and women.
When he feels more like drowning
Than gliding or swimming?

'Oh no!' you say because it's not true
You go there to do the stuff you do.
So what are the things that call you there?
Is it that old, rotting brown leather chair?
Or the radio with football or politics on?
Or the tools and claptrap that make you man?

The box of screws in many forms;
A variety of saws and hammers the norm.
Bits of wood and slithers of steel,
Oh how you love to feel...
A king amongst his kingdom of tools
No time for drama or nagging fools.

Shed Man O Shed Man
So oft you go
To your kingdom of tools
That calms your soul.

GONE FISHING

My man has gone a'fishing
He's off to catch some fish.
I wonder if he'll bring home sea bass?
Oh how do I wish.

He says he'll get some supper
On his way back from the lake,
But supper could be breakfast time
For the hours that he takes.

I wonder what he does
When he sits and casts his line
Does he suck on wiggly wriggly worms,
Or maggots all the time?

My man has gone out fishing.
Don't know when he'll return,
And I bet he forgets the supper tonight,
But least he ate some worms!

THE PUB

What is that place that draws you in?
A place of beer and roaring din?
A den of thieves or a smuggler's cove.
A place where men do love to go.

A secret club of macho stuff;
You never seem to get enough.
Of 'Going to the pub' my dear
And to me it is Oh so clear.

That the public house is just a place,
Where men can go to get some space
From home and work and all that strain
Before they venture home again.

A space where boys can meet their mates
A place where jokes can meet their fate.
Banter, fun and chortles reign
It seems to keep most men sane.

But some they've lost their space in life.
Maybe too much hardship and unwelcome strife?
For the pub has now become their home
Where the devil drink inside them roam.

BANTER

Oh you love to banter
Love to pull my leg
Like it when I roll my eyes
At a quip that you just said.
The roar of men a' laughing
When one has said a joke
Must be fun to be a man
When bantering with the blokes.

MY OH SO SECRET CLUB

I'm in a secret club
And I'm feeling oh so cool
It made up for all those awful times
I didn't get, included at my school.
My club it has a name
And a rolled up trouser leg
And I have to sit inside a box
And go dib dib to a guy called Greg.
My dad he had a club
For guys called Dave and Bob
And I know he would have said my club
Was for weird blokes without a...door handle

BOYS AND MEN

I love my boys I do
I love them with all my heart
They never moan if the lid's left up
Or even when I fart.

In fact they think I'm funny
And the grosser that I am
Makes me seem a kind of hero
Not some nambypamby lamb.

I love my mates so dearly
When we're hugging at the pub
Or when we hit the curry house
For some after drinking grub.

They don't care if I am loud
Or leave my shoes on in the house
And I can look at other girls
And not get called a turgid louse.

Ah I love all my best buddies
For I know they never judge
And if I'm drunk and too late home
Towards the taxi they will nudge.

WANNA BE HERO

So you wanna be a hero
And beat the baddies at their game?
To fly and fight and shoot those guns
And be called Arnie or a big 'ole name?

So you want to defeat Thanos
With all your Marvel gang?
And send him to another place
Where the bad guys all belong.

If you could be invisible
Or fly and shoot some web,
You'd be so loved by one and all
And never called a pleb.

Do all boys and men desire
To be the hero of their dreams?
To be more than just pure normal
And better than they seem?

But those superhero winners
Rarely live their life so sweet,
So enjoy the life you're given
And be the hero of your street!

NOBODY'S PERFECT

BARGAIN BUCKET BOB

Bob loves a bargain
He's 'Bargain Bucket Bob'.
He's really quite annoying,
In fact he's quite a... pain.

He hovers round the discounts
He's sniffing out the sales
He buys up all the gone off stuff
He thinks he cannot fail.

At car boots he'll have a punt
At knocking down that price
He's kinda really slimey
And isn't very nice.

But we love our Bargain Bucket Bob
With such affection so
Until he got the last cheap seat
Then he really had to go!

We played a little trick
It's naughty but it's true.
Where we booked him on the cheapest flight
A one-way bargain trip to sunny Timbuktu

DIY

You love a little tinkle with your nuts and bolts it's true.
Your tools they have a tool bag which you think is really
cool.
The saw it has a space inside your man made shed
And the screws have got a little home inside some
homemade beds.

Bits of wood and plastics all lay around the house,
But you can never find a pencil
And blame the secret mouse.

Lighbulbs for each and every shade
And batteries galore.
Tapes for things to measure
And hinges for the door.

Banging, clattering noises
When the weather is just fine,
Or fixing garden hoses
And things a' leaking all the time.

But alas when you are busy,
Or when footie's on the box
Or when you go a' hunting
With mates in coats to catch a fox.

Then the lights they all stay broken,
The garden hose don't work
And as for all those leaky things
It's just one big, nagging joke!

So I've found me Bob the handyman
He's really very sweet
He comes and fixes all the stuff
And lives just down the street.

He likes to taste my brownies
He loves to chat for hours
He even fixes things for free
And often brings me flowers.

I think that you have noticed
That this fella comes for tea
Cos you're fixing all my broken bits
And fussing over me.

So goodbye my handyman friend
You were lovely yes it's true
But the temptation to DIY your bones
Means it's goodbye from me to you.

FLUTTERING FINGERS

My man likes a flutter
He thinks that I don't know
But his gambling app leaves a trace
Like footprints in the snow.

The things he does in secret
A flutter here and there
And sometimes he comes up a winner
But oft the cupboard's bare

My fella likes the bookies
Although he would deny
But I've seen the way he hides receipts
And I often catch him cry

Bless my bloke with all his foibles
Damn that guy to hell
He's gambled all his money
And the house and car as well!

THE ONE THAT GOT AWAY

I coulda been a league man
And got myself some caps.
I shoulda been a teacher
With thirty in my class.
I woulda been a hero
If Marvel had met me.
I might have been a movie star
If taught by Scorcese.
I'm sure I'd have won the cup
If not left on the bench.
And I might have met a princess
If I hadn't met that wench.
I woulda coulda shoulda
Got the biggest single fish
And brought it home so you could cook
That woulda coulda been our dish.

THERE'S A MAN IN THE KITCHEN

Oh man in the kitchen making us grub
Using every single pot we have,
Can't wait for them to scrub.
My man is in the kitchen
And stuff is everywhere
Flour on floor, on worktops
And even on the chair.

Go man in the kitchen; cooking up delight
It's man in kitchen Tuesday.
I do it every other night.
I wonder what he's making?
I can guess that it must be
Pretty complicated for the ingredients that I see.

Four different types of cans
And a jar of something else
And every spice been taken down
From the spice space on the shelf.

There's steam and bubbles popping
And the oven's on full blast
And all I heard is 'Ow and Crap!'
How long will this all last?

Then just two hours later,
When the bottle has half gone
And I've made two calls,
Did a wash and sung the toddler a song.

Ah it smells delicious that gourmet meal for two
He's made it all so tasty and I smile in gratitude.
I do not look upon the chaos,

That he has left behind
For now I'll savour my lover's meal
And the wine will make me blind!

NAILS IN THE SINK

You left some in the bath
And some were in the sink.
Some had flipped onto the floor,
Quite a few of them I think.

One was on my toothbrush
And two on toilet seat.
I guess you must have been in a rush,
Or had slippery wandering feet!

You have a real poor aim,
And completely missed the bin.
And I know you used the clippers
For you still had one in them.

Why are they all so yellow,
With bits of ground-in dirt?
And you left them grow so long and hard;
Boy that must have hurt?

What sweet endearing treasures,
From my lover just moved in.
It's made me see a side to him,
That's really rather grim.

I think I'll write a little note
To get my point across

'Clip your nails outside
You rotten pig.
Your habits are just gross!'

DIRECTIONS

Do you know where we are going?
For it looks like we are lost,
But still we pootle on and on
And round and round that post.

You will not stop and ask,
For that is not your way.
Instead we drive for hours,
Losing half the day.

We both are getting rattled
And the kids all need a pee,
But still you will not relent,
So we find a tree to wee.

Only when the tank is low
Do you finally concede
To accept that wee small truth,
That we are lost indeed!

YOU GOTTA WIN

Second's not an option
Third is something gross
If you spin or throw the dice
You bet you cannot lose

Being best is awesome
Being first is sweet
Even if it's being first
To walk into your street

Scrabble is a nightmare
The words that you concoct
And though the word 'Quotzojmix
Is not a word
Somehow you do object.

Your mates are just the same
It's really quite bizarre
That you ooh and ahh and go all goosh
When one buys a flash sports car

Why are some men so obsessed
With being just the best?
And always being number one
And fingers up to all the rest?

INSTRUCTIONS

It came with an instruction
But still you didn't look
You said you knew just what to do
And didn't need a book.
You couldn't find your ruler
Or the pencil stuck behind your ear;
And that is why it took so long
Plus 5 cups of tea my dear.

Much later than expected
The thing was up and built
But we scratched our heads together
Because a bit that would not fit.

So you looked at the instructions
From A to B to Zed
And boy it took 3 more cups of tea
To reconstruct that bed!

SHORT MAN SYNDROME

Great things come in packages
Of all shapes and size and stuff
But some people have an issue
With not feeling quite enough.

Small does not mean invisible
Small is not a big, bad sin
So why do some short men and dogs
Create such a crazy din?

They shout and bark and fuss
It really isn't neat,
Just because they're five feet tall,
With tiny, little feet.

Their chest can go all puffy
And their face can get all red.
In rage and noise and anger,
For something not liked that was said.

It's the same with little dogs,
Who yap as though they were,
A Dane in all it's greatness,
Yet probably with much less fur.

So chill all you little people,
For women love cute men
And if your personality and heart are kind,
You'll pull them again, again and again.

NEVER WRONG MAN

Why won't you just admit it
That you made a big mistake?
No one's going to kill you
If the blame for it you'll take.
Come on man just say it.
That you were not right this time,
That you didn't get the answer right;
You cannot win it everytime.
But no you cannot say that.
You cannot say those words
'I'm sorry I was wrong my dear'.
Instead of, 'Me wrong? Ha! Don't be absurd!'

PANTS AND SOCKS

I love the way you decorate
The floor with all your stuff.
I thought you loved the new rug
But it doesn't seem enough
Although it's rather pretty
And it costs a fair bit too
You much prefer your own stuff
Despite those skids of poo.
The socks they land all random
And never seem to match
And your pants I can't go near
You're definitely a catch.
I've left out two big baskets
A hint to put things in
But then you go and drop your clothes
Besides the dirty washing bin!

LOO SEATS UP!

Decades worth of our words, seem not to influence you
On why the seat should be returned on every toilet loo.
Apart from being ugly, with the pan laid out so bare
The contents of your inards
Are so often witnessed there.

Marks and grime not counting
Or skidmarks in the bowl
It's a bone of our contention
And really makes us howl.

Men why do you do it?
Why do you not see?
That the lid goes down everytime
After you have had your pee.

Now it may not seem so important
In the global world of stuff
But it really drives us barmy
And we've simply had enough.

So please return your seat
When a tinkle you have had
And when you learn to master that,
Please inform your dad!

MR MULTITASKER

You say we cannot multitask
You say we cannot juggle,
More than one activity,
As it gets us in a muddle.
But this is just not true
As men are really great
At starting lost of different things
And finishing them way too late!

PRIVATE PARTS AND MAN MADE STORIES

THE POWER OF SIX

Is six the norm because you say so?
Is that after squats and touching your toes?
Couldn't find a ruler
And the tape measure's gone
But still you hum that crazy man song.
'Six is the norm and so I'm fine
Enjoy your six but first the wine.
I'll get you tipsy so you can't see
That six is a little exaggerated by me.'

APPENDAGES AND OTHER MAN MADE STORIES

Is it such a thing to want to have a big ole ding-a-ling?
To be engrossed by a thing,
That flops and hangs between your toes
Ok, that sits astride, under your nose.
No that's not right!
Otherwise you would have to fight,
With elephants and horses
And animals with
A huge appendage with length and girth
O but such mirth!
We laugh. And then we see the thing of the giraffe!
A myth that man could dangle
A thing between his legs and wrangle
Truth as though it were the norm
To say your thing has bigger form.

INVOLUNTARY ERECTIONS

Whoa there it goes! The tower erect
Standing up to attention in perfect defect.
Trying to hide evidence and traces,
Of my thing going firm in inappropriate places.
The woman's legs crossing
That button undone
Whilst just fleeting thoughts,
The sensation will come.
It starts in my head,
Rushing right down to 'it'.
Damn you appendage, you stuck little git!

HANDS DOWN PANTS

Are you searching for some treasure
Whilst enjoying a quick, fun fiddle?
Come on all you guys,
And answer me this riddle...

Why is it that some men,
Like their hands inside their pants?
Is there a good reason,
Or is it just by chance?

That they twiddle and they cuddle,
Whatever they can find
And then they smile in pure delight,
And sit with legs astride.

Oblivious and happy
Sitting whilst they hold,
Their cockles in deepest pleasure
The answer left untold.

THE RELEASE

Man Oh won't you tell me
Why Oh why it is?
That you think about 'it' all day
And then have to release?
How many times do you do it
It seems like quite a feat?
What is it with your need to go
Down that one way kinda street?
Even when you're married
Or loved up with someone sweet,
I hear you still like to bat your ball
Many times a week.
It's really very strange
And it's not something we could suss,
That a man has such an always need
Even when not with us!

IT

Obsessed with It
Thinking of It
Wanting It
Dreaming of It
Damn It
There must be more to life than It?

ROUNDHEADS AND CAVALIERS

This is a different kind of battle
Of which nobody really wins.
It's a preference and a taste
Like a choice of rum or gin.
But no matter what men go for
Or have it made for them,
Whatever type of hat they wear
They're real men all the same!

FANTASY BOY

Your head must hold some stories
Of places you would go
Of things you'd do and stuff you'd see
And pictures that you'd show?

But those fantasies go further
Than a bucket list in head
It seems they also venture
To the sofa, chair and bed.
The things you say you'd do
If given half the chance,
Not sure if I should be scared
Or do a crazy, whoop whoop dance!

And then you throw out names
Like I'm supposed to know
What each and every one is
And if there really is a dog in tow?

Spooning (does that involve cooking?)
Sofa Straddle sounds a strain
Cowgirl and then in reverse
Cowboy outfit once again?
The Lotus...ah a flower. Beautiful to see
Sideways and the Crab Walk?
Think I'd better make some tea.
Are Dogs required for the Doggy?
And is The Cross just for Sunday?

Oh my with all these choices
Can I have my little say?
I like it plain and simple
Not exhausting like some of those

When we snuggle close together
And things are touching, like our toes.
Missionary sounds great
But I'd really like to see
What you'd looked like as a nun
Now that's fantasy for me!

HOLES AND DONGLERS

If a man is a walking dongler
And a woman a hole in one,
What's the point of restaurant dates
And texting weeks by phone?

Why not greet each other
With just the in and outy bits?
Unless of course you're wanting more
Than that something in my nicks?!

SAUSAGES

I'm on a dating site, or two
And I'm feeling really rather blue
It seems so many guys
Take pleasure in their flies
Or more precisely the contents of
What can only be called a sausage log.

So many have I seen
And all are quite obscene
Sausages in all shapes and sizes
Some are flaccid and some in rises
But all are gross it must be said
Oh what goes on inside these guys' head?

Some carry chipolatas
Inside their bigger trousers,
And what a load of baloney
When it's as pale as a polony.
I might just do a run boy
If it's red just like a savaloy,
And not everyone can manage
Your Mr Jumbo Sausage.

So keep them to yourselves
Your butcher's pre-packed meat
Or you will be swiped to left not right
And I will rightly fleet.

MORNING GLORY

Waking up
Stab in back
Gone for wee
Return to sack
Cut down broom
Makes some room
Revenge is sweet
Go back to sleep

YOU KNOW THAT O?

It's not all about the O
Surely you must know?
There's more to it than O
You know.
You know that don't you know?

THE NAMES YOU CALL YOUR THING

Funny how a man
Likes to call his thing a name
Like a little pet he carries
In his trousers all the time

Weiner, shiner, Billy Bob
Any thing that rhymes with knob
John Thomas, Lord Hardwick
Womb Raider, Trouser Snake
Moby Dick and Rumpleforeskin
King Dong and Herman Von Longschlongstein
Then there's Roger the One Eyed Monster
Knobgoblin and Long Dong Silver.

Do you want me to go on?
Or can we agree to call him John?

UNWANTED PIC

If you think a woman,
Wants to really see
An inbox pinging pic
Of your shiny, male thingy?
Then you'd better think again
Cos it's never really cool
And it makes us laugh or vomit
Not rolling round in drool.

FOOT FETISH

So you love to hold a foot
And stroke along the top
Until it really tickles
And then you have to stop.

You love to suck a toe
It does something weird to you
And you are really kinda hoping
That I kinda like it too.

But I really have to tell you
I really must confess
That I would rather
Pick up your toenails
Than have my foot caressed!

STUFF YOU SHOULDN'T WATCH

So why do you?
Watch
Stuff you really shouldn't
On those naughty sites
After dark or alone
You sometimes use your phone
To make a call
To some strange voice
You don't have to, you know
You have a choice
To not watch or call
Or fall
Into that slippery place
Of porn

OTHER PARTS AND STUFF

THE BELCHER

Some sounds need to stay deep down inside.
Like crying for Mama on a big, scary ride.
Or cursing loud in front of the sprogs,
When you stub your toe hard, because of the dog.
Or a tickly cough when surrounded by people,
Or needing to fart when trapped in a meeting.
Like talking too loud in a quietened room,
Or not muting the sound for a meeting on Zoom.
Then munching some pretzels and rustling the bag,
Or mumbling out loud when your wife starts to nag.
Yes there are times when mouths should stay shut.
Zipped and locked up and done without fight.
For silence is golden at key times like these
And we know you can do it,
So we're begging.
Oh please!
Keep that gob shut,
When a belch loud and clear,
Rises forth from your gut
And right to my ear.
Be quiet and swallow that explosion in cheeks,
Or put hand to mouth,
To sound more like a squeak.
But instead you just look and let it all go.
The belcher has struck
And I run out the door!

BALD HEAD

Where does it go, all that hair from your head?
Do you cry when it falls, is it something you dread?
Is there a thief who comes and steals in the night,
And cuts off pieces of hair in delight?

Does the pillow pull out fluff from the roots,
Does shampoo have conspiracy shares at Boots?
One minute full the next minute bare
Where Oh where has it gone all your hair?

HAIRY BACKS

Some women love a hairy back,
Some women love bear chests.
Some women love to cuddle men
With more hair than on their own head.

A bear is kinda sexy,
To someone don't you know.
While others like their partner bald,
From neck right down to their toes.

It's just a case of preference,
It could be beautiful to see;
A hairy man with a hairy back
As long as there's no hairs on his knees!

HAIRY ORIFICES

When a man gets to a certain age,
When age does start to show,
He accumulates the weirdest fluff
In places you'd never go.
His ears whilst droop and lengthen,
Will also seem to grow
The strangest looking garden;
Stuff that really shouldn't show.
And then out of his nostrils,
Sprout a swamp of nasty things,
Attaching onto hairy ropes,
And hang out like darkened strings.
I think I saw his nipples once
And now I need a shrink
The curly hairs that sprouted forth
Really made me blink!
And then there are his toes
Oh my I must declare,
That I think I know where his head hair fell,
It seems they landed there.

MOOBS

It's ok to have them
Just don't know why they are there.
Is it a resting muscle thing,
Or something going spare?

Do you need a bra?
I think they do your size.
It might be just what you'll need.
It might be rather wise.

To uplift and to secure,
Those hanging softened mounds.
To stop them tickling tummy,
Or making flappy sounds.

Moobies we could call them,
Or Mockers sounds quite apt?
But rest assured, they're part of you,
So I am sure we'll adapt.

It's a fact that yours are bigger
Than mine could ever be.
Perhaps I should grow a donker
and stand up when I pee?

SCRATCHING...

I think I know why men have balls
And women's bits are in
If they didn't have those nuts to scratch
We'd lose them to the gym!

TOUPEES AND COMBOVERS

Your hair is getting thinner
For some it's just all gone
You're no longer feeling king
Without your hairy crown
So you go and get a piece
That attaches with a clip
And pray it isn't windy
Or the piece will do a flip.
And what if you have a few
Hairs still left high on top?
Do you get a little comb
And get it all to flop
Across one side to another
To make your head look like
A mouse has done a runover
On your head with his big ole bike.

BEARDS AND STASHES

A smooth shaved face
In just the right place
Like a Bond premier
Where it's right to go bare
Or presenting a meeting
No matter how fleeting
In well cut out attire
Makes the man look on fire.
Kissing the face of a man with no trace
Of stubbly growth
Or a stash under nose
Can seem oh so sublime
Time after time.

Though give me a beard
Cut close to the skin
A slither of stubble
Will welcome me in.
A rash I may get from the friction so close
To my own luscious soft skin
Ooooh give me a dose
Of a kiss from a man with a beardy face
Not someone with not one hair out of place.
But beware beardy guy for I have to declare
If a clean, shaven Bond came, then I'd settle for bare.

THE SOUND OF YOUR NOSTRILS PART 1

Your snoring keeps me up at night.
Not ghosts or ghouls or terror frights.
Not money woes or stressful cares,
Just your bellowing sounds of nostrils flared.

It wakes the cat, disturbs the dog,
Who without you home, sleep like logs.
The kids are woken with moans of 'Dad!'
When did your snoring get so bad?

Would I have stayed early on in,
When two lusty people made different sin?
When we slept so sound and spooned together,
Awoken only by Britain's stormy weather.

What was the thing that happened to you?
That makes me so wrecked and feeling so blue?
The bags that now hang beneath eyes that once shone;
Dark, wretched circles, proof of your song.

The one that keeps me up at night,
Where I leave the room and that's not right.
I lay with the dog and the cat snuggles in,
As we await dawn rise bemoaning your din.

THE SOUND OF YOUR NOSTRILS PART 2

Lights go out and wind has calmed
Night sets in and in your arms,
I ready for sleep.
Yet no sleep comes.
A train it starts to pull away
From a darkened tunnel at close of play.
A gentle whistle hums out a tune
Signals the state of play till dawn.
And then the train it chugs a little
Oblivious of its intermittent spittle.
Whistle, chug, whistle chug
On and on the train it rides
Whilst passengers watching, no place to hide.
Then someone pulled an inner brake
For an increase to the chug it makes.
And stop. Peace. A moment.
Then whistle, chug, whistle, chug
And I wish there was a drug.
That he or I could take
To stop his snoring or me awake.

HE WITH THE SWEET TOOTH

Sugar in your tea
Cake, the biggest slice
Half a pack of cookies
But heck they were so nice.
Always have a pudding
And crumpet with some jam
I'd love to have a flapjack please
After bagel filled with ham.
Christmas cake with custard
Or treacle sponge will do
And if you've got a bakewell tart
I'll have a slice with you.
But trifle is my fave
Just like my mother makes
But if it isn't like hers,
Just make sure you learn to bake!

AND ODE TO POO

AN ODE TO POO

Pooing is such sweet sorrow
Alas tonight's vindaloo is tomorrow's
Stuff in loo.
Too much meat creates mean feat
To extract from down under
And leaves you ponder
If salad one should partake
To solve this rock hard state

Oh pooing is such sweet sorrow
When faced with explosive matter
That rips out of orifice
And you are left to face
The bitter sweat and tears
Of rotten tummy fears

Alas pooing is sweetest sorrow
I had two today;
I'll have three tomorrow.

POO HUMP

I'm talking here of poo,
That stuff that's in the loo,
And men's fascination
With the length of their defecation.

But some men get poo hump
When checking on what they've dumped
And think their world has ended
When it slips around the U bend.

WINDY POPS

Is there a volcano that lives amid
The lining of your national grid?
That erupts at will and not at pleasure
Is far from sweet and not a treasure.
Just the sound withers my soul
And then I hear you scream out 'Goal!'
As the putrid gases reaches my face.
Really this is such disgrace.
You find it funny when I cough and splutter
Until I kick you in the nuts. Eh?!
And then you know how gross it feels
To smell your nasty gut-churning spills.

THE SOUNDS OF YOUR ANUS

Phewwwt and phoooo you let them rip.
Silently or loud they skip,
Out of your bellowing anus hole
Into the net of my nostrils.
Goal!
I know you silently scream,
As I less than silently wheal.
What do men eat that makes them gas
And release toxic waste from their hairy...butt?

THE STATE YOU'RE IN

THE PILL THAT YOU TAKE

Why do men take so many pills
For all their gripes and inner ills?
A pill for this and one for that
For pressure of blood, gout and helping of heart.
For bits and bobs and aches and pains
For making things work again
But the pill that we can never see
Is the pill that starts with the letter V!

MAN FLU

Behold there is mandemic!
It's global and it's here.
It's got red eyes, a grotty nose
And it's gone right off the beer.
The world is falling in,
He can't get out of bed
He thinks that he is dying
With a raging, pounding head.
He's got me on fetch and carry
And as servant maid to him.
So I've left him with a Beechams
And gone to buy some gin!

WHAT'S WRONG?

Tell me what's up, what's going on in your head?
These are words often said
From me to you
When I feel you're blue
It's true.

But alas you withhold
Any words to be told
Your secrets stay hidden
No speak to be given
Just silence.

Okay but not okay
Tell me another day
But another day does not come
And you?
Well, you,
Stay blue.

NOT ALRIGHT

Talk to me and tell me what's up
I can see that your cup
Is overflowing with nothing growing
Just mould and sticky yukky slimy stuff
That's eating up your soul
Driving you to a darkened hole
Don't go there
I swear.
I can help
Reach out to me or someone else
Stay on top, do not flop
Or fall
And fall.
Because you do not call.
Just call.

NUMBING THE PAIN

The waves that crash my brain
Over and over and over again
They won't go away.
Ignoring don't help
Hiding they seek
No joy in life
I just want to sleep.
Wave after wave after wave
They don't behave
So I then crave
The thing to numb the pain.
And when the pain is numb
And I have gone all dumb
I start again
To numb the waves and all that pain.

DOCTOR DOCTOR

It started with a pain
And then it got quite worse
We nagged for you to see someone
But you scowled and you cursed.
It didn't go away, even though you said it would
And though we nagged and nagged you still
Your brain it was like wood.

Finally you went and the doctor he was grave
He said you had been stoic, even venturing on brave
He sent you to the hospital
To get you done some tests
And that was just some months ago
And you were finally forced to rest.
The road was short and manky
With more bumps and lows than highs
But sadly when the pain had left
You were way up in the skies.

REAL MEN DON'T CRY

Cry boy cry, let it all out
Or else one day you will rage and shout
A hurting man once deprived of tears
Cannot let out the pain and fears
Not used to expressing such
It grows into mould and hurts too much.
So cry boy cry, let it all out
So one day you'll have less to shout about.

STICKY STUFF

Not it's not that other stuff
That your thoughts just went straight to.
I'm talking of the gloopy fat
That men are quite prone to

The chocolate and the cakes
The biscuits with their tea
And all that super naughty foods
That I see you eat for tea

But beware the ticking bomb
Inside your handsome chest
Where all the sticky fatty stuff
Gets stuck under your breast.

NEVER TOO OLD

NEVER TOO OLD

I may be edging ninety
And my knees are old and frail
And my heart may just be ticking
And my skin showing up its veins.

I'm pensioned and I'm lonely
Most of my friends have passed
And my memory may be fading
But I know I had a blast.

So when that lady walks in
At almost half my years
I do not think I am
A guy with drooping ears

Instead I see me twenty
With youth that's on my side
It's only when I wink at her
Do I realise I'm half blind

For the 'young lady' that I smiled at
And offered her the look
Was really a fella in a kilt
About to read his book.

MIDDLE OF NIGHT TINKLE

Around three
I need a pee
Just a little tinkle
To empty out my winkle.
Even if I starve it,
Like a desert with no rain,
Somehow my bladder fills right up
And I'm in toilet once again.

TWINKLY EYES

See that little twinkle
The one that's in my eye?
It's there because you think I'm past it,
Just cos time's gone by.
And although you see me aged
And think that I'm no catch,
My girl, inside I'm twenty-five
Now what do you think of that?

FALLING APART

Everything is failing
From my fingers to my toes.
My eyesight's poor, my mouth is dry
And there's a garden up my nose!

It takes a while to stand up,
And weeing's quite a feat;
Like waiting for the bus to come
And when it does, it's such relief!

My clothes are green and beige
As that's just now how I feel,
But my mind is still alert
And I remember yesteryear.

So don't discount me yet,
For there's life in this old dog,
But if I forget your name my dear,
It's something called brain fog!

GRUMPY AND OLD

In my day things were different
The old ways were much more blessed.
My father knew how to discipline
And my mother she knew the rest.
We didn't make a fuss
Didn't grumble very much
Got up, got dressed and went to work
And tried to do our best.
Beer was less expensive
And the butcher's knew my cut
Loved going to the barber's
And catching up with chat.
The kids were all polite
And respected elders so
Or else, they'd get a clip round ear
And if really naughty, two
We had the cheapest fun
It didn't cost a lot.
The days we spent in parks
And riverbanks and fields.
I got a broken arm
From swinging from a tree
But it hurt much less than Jimmy's
When skateboarding tore his knee.
Oh those were the days
You cannot bring them back
Life has gone to crazy street
And I get that that is that!

PART TWO
RELATIONSHIP, LOVE
AND
MISUNDERSTANDINGS

OF LOVE AND FRIENDSHIP

FRIEND ZONE

Some men are best as friends
Aren't meant to be your lover
They make you laugh
They listen for hours
And even like your mother!
But alas when they declare
Their hidden love for us
If feels just like the world's blown up
And we've fallen under a bus.
For when we have to friend zone
The thing you hate us do
It's then we have to face up
The end of me and you.
For you hate it when we say
'I only see you as a friend'
And for some real crazy reason
For you the friendship ends.

AN ODE TO THE MAN FRIEND

What is a woman without her male mates;
Especially when single,
And no sign of a date?

What is a lady without an escort,
When no lover has she
And no love options of sorts?

What is a belle without her Beast,
Who picks her up when she's down
Makes her giggle at least?

What is a Piglet without her loyal Pooh,
With no free male woodland creatures,
What then should she do?

She makes a call to you
The guy she calls her mate;
That's what she will do,
If she doesn't have a date.

She tells you all her secrets
And never quite holds back
You get to see her all dressed up,
Or in Pjs in her sack.

She can talk to you bare faced,
Without a hint of rouge
And she even talks on Facetime,
When peeing on the loo!

She cries when you are looking.
She laughs till she gets hoarse
And she'll trust you with her life.
You should know this truth, of course.

So don't you go and blow it,
By giving sex a shout
And asking if she'll be your gal,
Or even ask her out.

SOUL MATE

I was nine and you were ten
You liked my mate whose name was Ben
But I was smitten right on that spot
With a pretty nine year old called Dot.

Years went by and so did you
Your parents moved to a place called Crewe
Teenage times distracted well
That I missed a girl from Holywell.

Uni came with Freshers Fun
Beers and gals before it began.
And then I saw the fairest sight
My schoolgirl crush one Friday night.

My heart it skipped and skipped some more
As I sidled up beside the door
Where you were stood beside a friend
Another male. Could I contend?

I cannot recall the words I said
For fear had placed me in sweet dread
Time had not changed my love for you
That kind, cute girl from Junior school.

Alas you did not jump right in,
For you had a guy whose name was Finn
Months they dragged as I had to wait
Until Finn was dumped for our first date.

And that was sixty years ago
And so I want for you to know.
That as I hold your hand to pass
Love like ours will always last.

FOREVER LOVE

The first moment we met I knew
You were the girl for me
Instinctive connection
My heart's re-direction
To only you, but you didn't see.

Life was unkind and so was your ex
He didn't understand love, just lust.
How lost you became and there you stayed
And as your other strayed
In I walked.

Into your life.
Patient
Loving.
Tender
Giving
Only friendship.

Until you could see
The love for me
That I already held for you
And now we are two.
Forever in love

ONE KISS

Great night, coffee, beers and wine
Holding hands; so sublime.
At door we stand and look
Like something from a Disney Princess book.
Your eyes find mine and I am caught
Lost in a moment no other thought
Than to slowly lower to touch
Those lips all night I've wanted much
And then we do
And I am lost in you.
Soft, wetness, perfect oneness
Marshmallow melting tongueness.
Ahh. Momentary bliss.
The one and only with you kiss.

CHATTING UP THE VINES

Do you come 'ere often
Never heard that before
Or the one that said
'My heart is knocking at your door'.
I throw the book of lines at her
And buy her a large gin
She smiles ever so politely
Cos she'll never let me in.
The night it gets so late
And I'm gagging for a date
When in you walk
And my heart talks
And I know that it is fate.
I sidle up beside you
Before another does
And I throw you all my best dart lines
To arrow out your heart.
And then my whole self withers
As you manly say to me
Oh darling thanks for chatting me up
But I'm taken for you see.
And see I do for sure
As I follow up your gaze
And my eyes fall right upon
The butch girl in the haze
I guess I have to get
Those glasses once prescribed
For I somehow pulled me a girl
That was more groom than was bride!

THE KNIGHT

I am a knight upon a horse
My steady stead leads me on course
To win fair maiden of the land
And beg her father for her hand.
Flowers I bring and gifts galore
I shall leave them upon her door.
And when fair maiden sees my face
Hers will light up with fullest grace.
For I have come to ride to her
And be the knight who steers her clear
From the hellish fate that life bestows
On who is born into life's deep woes.

But alas young maiden get a grip
No knight will come on such a trip
Romance is not dead but fairy tales yes
Enchanted fables just depress
Be your own Queen, so a king can come
To hold your hand and pinch your bum.

IT'S A MAN THING

NO MORE MR NICE GUY

Nice guys don't always win first place
Being just nice don't earn that space.
Why you cry?
I'll tell you why
Because though nice, we often try
To please and please far too much
And then we get kicked, into touch
And rage inside us bubbles up
Until an overflowing cup
Explodes and then there is a mess
And we are left to rue and stress
Because we did not win the race
In fact we come in near last place.
Bad guys may hurt and run a mile
And oozed you in with knowing smile
They get the girl and then dismiss
Her with a shag after the kiss
But nice guys no, they don't do that
They are sweet and kind
And that's the wrap
They give and give until it's gone
And then internally think they're wronged.
You did not give enough to me
And now I'm lacking can't you see?
I gave you all that you could want
And still it was just not enough.
I am feeling deep inside of me
A fuse of fire that slowly seethes
For all the times that I was wronged
And a feeling that I did not belong
And used I feel and that's not right
And so internally I fight
You think I'm crazed and stand aghast

When finally, I crack and blast
And damage all that was good to see
Cos nice guys lose and that was me.

BRINGING HOME THE BREAD

Bringing home the bread
He's bringing home the bread
He isn't very happy
But he's bringing home the bread

He's winning at the war
He's winning at the war
With his craggy boss and failing car
But he's winning at the war

He's feeling rather sad
He's feeling rather sad
But please just keep on going
Cos you're bringing home the bread.

YOUR MOTHER

It seems I got a mummy's boy
A real mother's lad
I thought he was so sweet and kind
The boy that I just had
Alas the cracks they shone
When I was invited round for tea
And then I saw that perfect guy
Was not the one for me.

Your darling, loving mother
Birthed that sweet boy of mine
Who she sees with tinted glasses
Not just some, but all the time.
She isn't giving up
Those tightest reigns on you
In fact I swear they didn't cut
The umbilical connecting her to you.

You see when you weren't looking
When you went to fetch the plate
She glowered cold and nasty
And said something mocked in hate.

'He loves his mother dearly
He comes round every day
He needs me very much
Since his father went away.
He seems to really like you
But I have high expectations dear
So if you want to stay with him,
You'd better draw me near.
It's me he really loves
You will never win first place

So if you do not mind that truth
I'll let you say the grace.'

MY MOTHER VERSUS YOUR MOTHER

I cannot even go there for you are sure to win
That little game of my mum's best
Though I love mine all the same.

Your mum makes all the best cakes
And her washing smells divine
She only has a Christmas tipple
Not like my mum's bottle of wine.

She is the best at cleaning
And her trifle tops the chart
Her gravy's fab, her roasts are hot
And you never hear her fart.

She always knows the answer
To everything it's true
And she gives the best hugs ever
Even better than mine to you.

But she doesn't have your baby
Like ours inside of me
She cannot go that far it seems
So that's one nil then to me ☺

COFFEE

First date coffee shop
What should for him I buy?
He's running late for our date
Polite, I do not ask him why.
He quickly texts when at my request,
What type of drink that I can buy.
'Coffee please and see you soon',
Came his hastened back reply.

Oh boy I cry.

Cappuccino, expresso, American, latte,
Flat white, galato, doppio, red eye,
Cortado, lungo, something called affrogato,
Macchiato, galão, Irish, Frappuccino,
Nitro, iced and café au lait.
That's when I silently swear.

Can a coffee bought impress?
Is it worth all this distress?
'Can I help you?' says the girl
Aarghh my head is in a whirl!

Tea. Earl grey.
Easy for me to say.
Anything else?
Yes!
Eyes lock. Hers and mine

Keeping her waiting isn't fine.
What to do, what to pick?
Why can I not choose one quick?

Then in he swoons and heart it skips a beat
Not for his looks, but from saving me defeat.
What coffee? I ask wiping my brow.
Black for me says he, for now.

AN ODE TO 40

Thirty eighty, thirty nine…
Counting time until the big 4-OH
Oh no!
The clock it struck
Me on the head
And the thirty something me is dead.
Time to re-inflate some life into these legs
To kick myself out of life's bitter, boring dregs
And get me some new,
But alas without you,
Or maybe with you too?
Can I have a little flutter on the side
With someone not my bride?
That new girl in the office
Young and without stress.
A quickie on the side.
I could hide.
Perhaps.
Yet so much that I could lose
By straying like a wanton cat
To get me some, a piece of that.
My ego cries out 'Go man go!
You're getting old at forty now.'
And yet I battle and despair
For I really do not want what's there.
A flicker of a touch, a feeling that I am much
Much more than I have become.
Is it worth it for a nubile bum?
To lose so much that we built up
Because I feel the empty cup
Of my current life.
Oh I do despair and lay awake at night
With this bitter mid aged fight.

And in the morning I wake up
And do declare
That I will buy myself
A shiny, flashy red sports car.

MID LIFE WAR

This space that I am in, what is it?
These clothes that I wear, whose are they?
I speak a language I do not understand
And walk a path I no longer want to walk.
What is the point?
Where is my essence?
Of who I am?

Provider? Yes
Lover? Yes
Father? Yes
Worker? Yes
Brother, son, grandson, cousin? Yes

But I am more. Much more.
And yet I do not know how much more there is to go.
So I am going. Somewhere.
Someplace. Somewhere else.
There is a war inside my soul
And though I fight to win
Something's I am sure to lose.
The spoils and chaos of war.
And this war will spoil
That which I have been
And may have yet become.
But to battle I must go
And you will cry I know.
So in both hope and sorrow do I go.

THAT ONE JOKE

It was funny the first time
Humorous the next
I think I had a giggle when the third time came by text.
The forth we were in company
And the fifth you were quite drunk
But the sixth to tenth was no excuse
Is it time for a new joke?

DAD ISSUES

When I said I do to you
I did not know that he came too
The shadow of a man not met
And yet
He lives within the cracks of you
And pours out grime and slime
And ugly goo
And eats the man that you became
And takes you back to a childhood game
That I do not know but feel I do
I got you both when I got you.

DO YOU SEE ME?

Not one of the cool guys who hang around at school
With flicky, floppy hair and a ciggie to look cool.
I blush when you walk past
And I often trip my feet
And I sometimes cross the road
When I see you in the street.

I'm spotty and I gangle,
Cos my lanky limbs all dangle
And I am not so good at sports
But at science I am tops
But I guess that doesn't make me cool
As king of science flops.

But I'd love for you to see me
This awkward looking boy
Who really wouldn't treat you
As some right of passage toy
Maybe one day I'll get some courage
To try to talk to you,
But until that day will come,
I'll be that awkward geek at school.

SPIDER-MAN

You cannot hate the creepers
Or the things that crawl the walls
You mustn't hide from mice and rats
That just won't do at all

And if a burglar comes a' knocking
You'd better knock him out
And if a fella goes and grabs my bum
Will you grab him and give him a clout?

But really if you see
A huge black hairy spider
With teeth and eyes and hairy legs
You'd better get beside her

I will not sleep at night
And I will so get the hump
If you do not get rid of it
That scary, hairy lump!

BETTER DRIVER

I'm a better driver of that there is not doubt
For I can reverse park and never have to shout
To the man beside the pavement
Minding his own stuff
To help you steer the car in
For you alone and not enough
To get that beast up straight
And lining up the kerb
I rest my case fair maiden
Because 'reverse park' is a man only verb.

AN ODE TO DAI

Dai the Bread and his van
Selling all things from biscuits to jam
When all is said and all is done
Dai the bread bless him,
Was a good, good man.

One Arm John
Walked the streets
Selling tickets for charity meets
With a slight little wobble and a little wheezy.
One Arm John that smiley geezer,
Lived a life less than easy.

Len the Coal
Funny old chap
Walking along, would suddenly stop
To pick up a coal piece from the street
Len the Coal pocketing coal and thinking it neat
Crazy guy, far from sweet.

Derek the Drink
Need we say more?
Drunk so much booze
Slopped on the floor.
Makes you think,
RIP Derek the Drink.

MISUNDERSTANDINGS

AND

UNDERSTANDING

DOES MY BUM LOOK BIG IN THIS?

Yes.
Er no.
Oh I don't know.
Perhaps.
Oh hell no.
No matter what I say,
I'm going to upset her.
Er, fancy going out for supper?

TIME OF THE MONTH

If you see me hiding
Or coming home quite late
Please do not be worried
That I've found some other mate.

It's just that I have noticed
That at a special time of month
You get real kind of nasty
Especially with your mouth.

Everything is slammed
And nothing's ever right
You think you doubled twice your size
Really? Overnight?

You say your skin is awful
And your hair it is a mess
And if I reassure you,
Our relationship's at test.

So I think it's altogether better
If I just stay away
Just a few days of your hellish time
Means we've twenty-six days left for us to play.

RED DRESS BLUE DRESS

Gotta choose a colour
If I don't we won't be out
But I am in dilemma
For giving one a shout.
If my mouth it opens wide
To choose a colour dress
I might be causing more harm
And more time-consuming stress.
Why do women ask us
What clothes that they should wear
We never seem to make the choice
That they really want to hear.

So instead I learned a trick
That I'll impart to you
To say you look damn fine whatevs
And say you need the loo!

SHOPPING WITH MY GAL

You bought yourself a dress; blue with lots of flowers
It wasn't an instance choice, I think we looked for hours.
Then sitting on a chair as you tried on a few more things
My head it did a double take
As I was next to the bras and nothing strings.

My eyes they couldn't help it
As I glanced at all the bits
The lace and cotton two-bit piece
That covered all size of...breasts.

To the right of my boggled eyeline,
Were the silky all-in ones
And I couldn't help but feel a blush
As a lady fingered one.

Then when our eyes they locked
And I couldn't help but flush
She gave me such a withered stare
I turned my head in such a rush.

Couldn't face another lady
Take a look at me
So my eyes instead they landed
On the stocking fillers tree.

Oh boy how I did wither
When a woman walks right out
Just in her bra and panties
Calling 'Miss?' in full girl shout.

And no matter where I looked
There were women everywhere
I didn't know what to do,
So sat in blush and full despair.

A warning to all men
When shopping with your spouse
Do not sit upon a lingerie chair
In fact do not leave the house!

PET NAMES

Baby, bae, babe, hey
Sexy, beauty, chickee, cutie,
Honey, bunny, tottie, hottie,
Pooh Bear, fluffy, cuddly wuddly,
Bubbles, cuckoo, Birdie, Welshie
Shorty, Buttercup, Lovey Dovey.
Dream girl, honey pie, precious, sunshine,
Lovely, beautiful, gorgeous, darling,
Love bug, pumpkin, apple of my eye
Beloved, doll, snookums, sweets,
Sugar, sweet pea, sweetheart, peach.

So many words from you to me
But baby hunny, can't you see?
I have a name so call me that,
Unless you've two of us?
And there's the catch!

WHY DO YOU WANT FLOWERS?

I bought you a diamond when you said I do
I bought you a house with an en-suite loo.
I bought you a car bigger than the drive
I gave you kids. In fact, you had five.
I took us on holidays and some first class
I even bought irrigation to clean out your...backside
Christmas you got Tiffany and some sparkling new things
Because I love you baby and know that you love bling.
A puppy came a knocking and you were oohs and ahhs
And I even bought you knockers
When you complained of your small bra!
But it seems all that I do
Just isn't quite enough
Because just yesterday,
You went off in a huff.
It was our eighteenth year, of saying yes I do
And although I bought a real sweet gift
Of love from me to you,
You somehow screamed the house down
Implied it weren't enough,
That you really didn't want
All that materialistic bling and stuff.
It seems this thing we got
This special love of ours
Can only really be expressed
If I buy you lots of flowers.

A BROKEN PERSPECTIVE

THE PROMISES YOU MADE

My father was the first to let me down with all his lies
The way he promised this and that,
Including one day that we would fly.
Then came Mr Right of Passage
Now he really was a card
But at seventeen you cannot help
For whom you fall so hard.
I was clued up after that
And left before they got
Lazy with their promising tongue
And all their useless, made up rot.

But ahh the years went by
And I thought that I was right,
Until in walked Mr Smooth
One cold November night.
How he made me giggle
And then swept me off my feet
He bought me meals; we drunk too much
And life felt pretty neat.
Compliments were flooding
And I felt just like a Queen
Until I realised that he had another
And it left me feeling green.

Darn those wayward truths
And all those promised things
If I could, I'd round the bad boys up
And scythe off their ding a lings!

ARE YOU LISTENING?

Why are you mutton when secrets I tell?
When my tears pour out from a deepened dark well.
When my soul has to vomit out all of my stuff,
When you're trying to keep up but it's really quite
tough.

Did you hear me? And all of the things I just said?
Or did the words fall down and melt into lead?
For your eyes have glazed over and you nod at strange
times
As you glance over my shoulder at the programme on
crime.

My mother is ill, did you listen to that?
Or even the news that the dog shagged the cat.
A volcano erupted just down the street
And the gout you have got means they'll cut off your
feet!

Yes yes you reply with a distracted nod to
Me who is standing just in front of you.
Can I buy a new bag my old one is old
With you so oblivious, I'm cunning and bold.

Yes yes you reply with a distracted nod to
Me who is standing just in front of you

BAD BOYS

The ones that always break your heart,
Are the ones that draw you near.
They give you what you think you want,
Then fill your heart with fear.
They swoop you off your feet
With attention just for you
And all the women love him;
We know this for you say it's true.
Something in his look,
The way he stands and what he says;
Maybe he has some tats
And leathers and he swears?
Or is it because he's clever
And knows how to win your heart?
And when the conqueror wins his prize
He swiftly will depart.

ONE IS NOT ENOUGH

One is not enough,
It does not fill you up.
Can you not feel just like a king,
With just the one small cup?
Does your crown it needs a polish?
If so, it cannot be by I,
For I am Queen and cannot bend
To this token king on high.
You say you cannot help it see,
That you have those boots to fill,
And sometimes your needs go crawling,
Into some other neighbour's spill.
Did she look so fine and dandy,
When she wavered past your nose?
It doesn't really matter, as she wasn't yours to choose.
You say you cannot help it,
That one is not enough,
And to please forgive you darling,
If you offer me one up.

GEEZER

He's a geezer
He's a teaser
A loser
A pleaser
Not
For he cannot
Think outside the box
For he is a fox
Sly not wry
He will not cry
Unless it's wolf
If you say bye.
That geezer.
Yes him
The less than women pleaser.

CRAZY LOVE

I'm crazy in love and broken in two.
I'm just a fool, crazy for you.
Watching you leave and holding the door,
But my heart lies shattered in pieces on floor

Turn around, look back, see my pain
And grasp my childish arms again.
Forget what isn't, forgive, let go;
Don't want to feel this hurt no more

You say you just grew tired
Of this thing that has no name,
And so I know this thing to you,
Was just a foolish game.

You didn't play the rules,
You played it your own way
And I didn't say a word of truth
And so I'm losing you today.

FRAGMENTED PIECES

I wasn't whole but kinda set,
No wobbly or fragmented pieces, yet.
The safe little me that knew my name
Only playing my own life game.

Then I met you and that longing was gone;
A fragrant mist; a forgotten song.
My sleep had thoughts of another's breath,
Of another's arms clasped over this beating chest.

Awakened moments, with you in my head
Meant life was joyous and longing was dead.
Purpose and meaning flooded through these veins
As love filled my drought-parched heart again.

Then quick as you came, the wind swept you away,
Like Old Mother Hubbard I sobbed for a day;
Which turned to a week and then some weeks more.
No more messages, or your face at my door.

My heart suffered most from this sudden withdrew
It flooded at first with tears that dried, as grief grew.
Then out of the pain it shrivelled a little,
Turned pale and sickly, withdrawing to spittle.

Then it dried and it splintered and tore clean in two
And remains fragmented pieces of a love not so true.

AND FINALLY...

Although I am no expert,
No scientist am I;
I must confess that I worked real hard,
In fact I tried, I really tried.
To understand the workings
From a woman's point of view,
Of what it must be like
To be a man like you.

So many ways we differ
This book shows just a few
From the things we do and like
To the toilet seat in loo.
I admit we need each other
To seed this human race
And maybe hold each other's hand,
To walk our century space.

I add a note to that,
For I think it must be said.
That it was pretty tiring thinking,
As a man inside his head.
And though some men think more like women
And some women more like men,
If I had to do this life once more
I'd come back as me again.

Paula Love Clark

Acknowledgements

Thank you to all the men I have ever known, be you family, friends, acquaintances or lovers. You were either an observation, a blessing or a lesson.

Special thanks to my friends Jason OB and John C for your patience with reading the poems, helping with edit suggestions and giving them your approval.

And finally thank you to my friends and family for humouring my poetic expressions.

Printed in Great Britain
by Amazon

49362588R00079